Preacher's Elect

UNIQUELY MANDATED BY GOD TO PREACH THE GOSPEL.

Preacher's Elect
UNIQUELY MANDATED BY GOD TO PREACH THE GOSPEL
Copyright © 2022 Debbieann Reid

All rights reserved.

Although the author have made every effort to ensure that the information in this book was correct at press time, the author does not assume and hereby disclaim any liability to any party for any loss, damage, or disruption caused by errors or omissions, whether such errors or omissions result from negligence, accident, or any other cause.

This book is not intended as a substitute for medical advice of physicians. The reader should regularly consult a physician in matters relating to his/her health and particularly with respect to any symptoms that may require diagnosis or medical attention.

No parts of this book may be reproduced in any form or by any electronic or mechanical means, including information storage in retrieval systems, without written permission from the author, except in the case of a reviewer, who may quote brief passages embodied in critical articles or in a review.

All scripture references used in this book were taken from the Holy Bible, Common English Version and can be found at http://thebiblegateway.com.

Editor: Crystal S. Wright

ISBN: 979-8-9860947-6-2

10 9 8 7 6 5 4 3 2 1
Printed in the United States

Priceless Publishing®
pricelesspublishing.co
Lauderhill, Florida

Contents

Acknowledgement 2
Dedication..4
Introduction 6
Chapter 1: My Story 9
Chapter 2: The Narrow Gate..15
Chapter 3: The Correction of Love...............................20
Chapter 4: Preachers vs. Pastors..................................25
Chapter 5: A Divine Call to Be Separated.....................29
Chapter 6: The Do's of Preaching................................34
Chapter 7: The Don'ts of Preaching.............................39
Chapter 8: The Authentic Preacher 52
Chapter 9: Never Compromise Your Anointing 60
Chapter 10: The Importance of Faith 64
Chapter 11: Graced to Complete, Not to Compete 69
Chapter 12: Ministry Tools: How to Handle Conflict & Affliction 73
Chapter 13: Breaking the Cycle of Church Hurt 78
Chapter 14: Showcase the Character of God 84
Chapter 15: Which Church Are You? 88
Chapter 16: Avoid Getting Burnt Out 90
Prayer to Activate God's Divine Will in Your Life............93

Acknowledgement

I give great glory and honor to the Holy Spirit who is the Author of this entire book. I am just the co-author. It is the Holy Spirit filled me with wisdom, knowledge and understanding, and gave me great revelations to write this book. I give Him thanks. Along the journey towards completing this book, God sent many other angels to help me. I will take this opportunity to acknowledge them here.

I thank **Dr. Sidjae Price**, who the Lord has used as an instrument to inspire and motivate me even when I wanted to quit. Thank you for your forbearance with me even when I resisted.

Prophetess Corieta McGlashen and **Natalee Folkes** — except the Lord had revealed it to you, you wouldn't have known about the existence of this book. Thank you praying for me and for the prophetic release for me to move forward with the vision.

To my friend and sister of the same faith **Simone Anglin**: thank you for always supporting and pushing me with all my endeavors, especially this book. Words aren't enough to let you know how much I love and appreciate you. Thank you for being my friend.

To my cousins and Pastors, **Pastor Kyle** and **Prophetess Monique Henry**: thank you both for your generosity, your selflessness and your continued support. Thank you for always making yourselves available to be used by the Holy Spirit.

In loving memory of **Maxine Flemming**: thank you for supporting and believing in me. Thank you for the many late-night prayers and conversations about this book. Thank you for motivating and encouraging me to pursue my vision of becoming an author. This is just the beginning of many great books to come.

Many thanks to my family and friends, and to everyone else who has supported me. Thank you very much for your love, encouragement and your perpetual support.

Last but definitely not least, I would like to honor and thank each and every one who has labored with me in preaching the Gospel. To everyone who has taught, ministered, imparted, and has travailed with me: thank you for devoting yourself in carrying out the assignment of pushing me into purpose. I assure you that your work is not in vain.

I give God glory for you all!

Dedication

God has released a SPIRITUAL diplomatic sanction to get the church back in order.

Preacher's Elect is dedicated to the entire body of Christ but specifically to the ones that are elected by God to preach the Gospel of Jesus Christ. God is calling every preacher — both installed and uninstalled alike — to a place of deliverance, correction and accountability.

Every one of us has something on the inside of us that we must contribute to this world. Ultimately, only what we do for Christ will last. It is up to us to tap into our inner self and pull it out, so that we can use it to the glory of God. We cannot just be a Preacher in name and not adhere to the responsibilities and divine expectations of the role.

I believe that through this book, the Lord is summoning those who He has elected and called to preach the undiluted word of truth. The state of the ecclesia is in danger of God's judgment. It requires an immediate response to the Lord's forbearance for us to be converted from a life of sin and mediocrity, to one of holiness and wholeness. God has released a diplomatic spiritual sanction to get the church back in order.

The *elect* refers to people who are chosen or singled out. As an elect, you should know that you were a part of God's plan before the foundation of the world, to carry out this great assignment of being a preacher. Simply put, God did not make a mistake, or guess when He chose you. You were chosen on purpose, for purpose, to do His will. This is why God is taking extreme measures to ensure that nothing interrupts His divine plan.

In this book I will share some visions and dreams that God has given me concerning the Preachers in His church. I will also share do's and don'ts of being an effective and submitted Preacher. My goal, as I believe God has mandated, is for you as a Preacher to come into alignment with God's will for your assignment, or go deeper in God in order for you His Holy Spirit to accomplish more through you. God cannot be exhausted. There is always more to do and accomplish for Him.

I encourage you to read this book with an open mind, and know that I write it firstly in obedience and secondly in love. May you be blessed, edified and rejuvenated by the Holy Spirit as you journey through these pages.

Introduction

This is the word of the Lord that came to me in a series of visions in 2019 for me to write this book. Being full of the spirit I was led to the book of Amos in the third chapter and the first verse, where God sent Amos to warn the people of Israel to repent and turn from their wicked ways.

> *Hear this word, people of Israel, the word the Lord has spoken against you — against the whole family I brought up out of Egypt: "You only have I chosen of all the families of the earth; therefore, I will punish you for all your sins." Do two walk together unless they have agreed to do so? Does a lion roar in the thicket when it has no prey? Does it growl in its den when it has caught nothing? Does a bird swoop down to a trap on the ground when no bait is there? Does a trap spring up from the ground if it has not caught anything? When a trumpet sounds in a city, do not the people tremble? When disaster comes to a city, has not the Lord caused it? Surely the Sovereign Lord does nothing without revealing his plan to his servants the prophets.* **Amos 3:1-7 (KJV)**

In this Spirit-led guide, the Lord is especially reaching out to those of whom He has elected and called to vigilant stewardship of His Church. The gospel of Jesus Christ and the kingdom of heaven must be preached. Therefore, it is imperative that those who are mandated by God to preach the gospel must do so vigilantly and diligently, in an out of season. **Preacher's Elect** serves as a guide to every elected preacher so you may be effective in doing the work that YOU have been called to do.

I humbly submit that God Himself has scripted these instructions to His elected ones because He cares for the well-being of all of His sheep and his shepherds alike — even the ones that are still wandering! Preacher's Elect is a mandated and unprecedented book that was penned and scripted by the Holy Spirit and directed to the Preachers that are chosen by God. Herein lies the instructions He gave me concerning His people.

God chases and corrects those whom He loves *(See Hebrew 12:6)*. Because we are loved and chosen by Him, He chastises us so that we won't harm ourselves and others. He does not want us to perish, so He always sends warning before He sends destruction.

Those of us who are parents can relate to this strategy, in that we regularly warn our children of potential danger, and offer them guidance on how to avoid it. Often, the children are unaware of the danger we warn them of, but our greater wisdom and experience allow us to see it clearly. Our love for our children motivates us to want to protect them.

However, we also have an obligation to correct them when they are in disobedience and rebellion. It is an immature and short-sighted child who cannot appreciate this privilege and gift of loving guidance. True love corrects and chastises when necessary. The Lord desires for us to avoid future destruction and that we steward well the anointing and charge that He's given us as Preachers.

CHAPTER 1:
My Story

I did not come from a religious background, nor do I come from a family line of theologians. I have no success story to tell. I lived a pretty basic life. I was born in Jamaica and raised by my grandmother who was a widow. She loved and trusted the Lord. We had devotions in the mornings and we prayed every single night before bed.

She used to take me to work with her. Her place of employment was a small shop in a market where she sold arts and crafts to tourists. I watched her witness to every customer she met, regardless of their race or nationality. We sang hymns and gave praise to God throughout the day. So, it wasn't a surprise to me that I was later ordained as a marketplace minister/chaplain pastor.

I was so blessed that she had planted the seed of righteousness in me from a young age. She taught me about the love of God and how He gave His only begotten son, Jesus Christ, as a sacrifice for us so that we can be saved. As I grew older, I started seeking a deeper knowledge of God. I wanted to understand my relationship with God. What was I to Him? Why did He make such a sacrifice for me? Why did He love all of us the way he did?

As I sought the Lord for the revelation, I learned more about God's sovereignty, the sacrifice of Jesus Christ and the presence of Holy Spirit in me. With that knowledge, I became more accepting of my priesthood. I could tell from an early age that I was different. Talking about Jesus wasn't very popular in Brooklyn, New York in the late '90s.

I was often mocked by my peers because of the passion and love I had for Jesus. But that did not bother me because I remembered the scripture that my grandmother taught me in Matthew 10:33. This scripture encouraged me and convicted me that I should be careful to not reject Jesus. This scripture taught me the fear and the love of God at the same time.

I grew up very bold in talking about Christ and expressing my love for Him to others. I would often have dreams about different things that were so frighteningly accurate. I still get goosebumps now when I remember them. Sometimes, I would get dreams about my friends and I would excitedly tell them about it. Often, it would play out in front of them in the exact way I had dreamed, and this made them look at me as if I was cursed. They would call me names and say that I was jinxing them.

So, for a very long time I shut down and would not speak of anything I had dreamed. I despised the ability to see things ahead, especially when it was a sign of danger or a warning of any sort. I was afraid of being rejected and ridiculed. I did not consider my gift to be able to see and hear things in the spiritual realm as anything special, I did not even think that God could use me.

Even though I was very popular in my early teenage years, I was an introvert. I often felt like an outcast and would prefer to be alone. I thought no one understood me. It wasn't until after many failed attempts at rejecting my calling, that I finally decided to surrender to the will of God for my life.

It is one thing when others do not believe in you nor see what God sees in you, but you should believe in yourself. I did not follow this advice for me for a very long time. I ran! Afflicted with the spirits of rejection and abandonment I was lost and confused; I ran. Then one day my life changed suddenly!

I received a very devastating phone call. It was the mother of one of my very good friends. She told me that he had died tragically. She asked me to read the eulogy at his funeral. I wrote a very emotional speech about the type of person he was and some of the fondest memories that I had with him.

On the day of the funeral when it was time to read the eulogy, I walked up to the front of the church where my friend lay in his casket. I was suddenly so frightened by the scene that I was unable to speak. My eyes became so filled with tears that it became impossible for me to read what I had written.

As soon as I was able to gather myself, a peace came over me that I cannot explain. I opened my mouth and the Spirit of God filled me up and began to speak through me. I cannot remember verbatim what I said, but I remember saying how I've always pictured myself preaching in front of a crowd but I never imagined it would be at my friend's funeral.

I thought to myself how could something so unthinkable happen to him? He was such a great person! I quickly realized that it could've been me lying there in that casket instead of him, so I cried out to the Lord and urged the patrons to give their lives to Jesus.

When I got off the altar and went back to my seat an older lady said to me, *"Little girl! You had your mother in tears. There wasn't a dry eye in the room while you were there speaking."* She continued to tell me that the entire church had been in tears —both young and old.

It was a bittersweet moment for everyone — bitter because we were saying goodbye to a loved one, but sweet, because we felt the presence of our Comforter in the room. I knew right then and there that I was called to preach. After the funeral friends and family gathered at the home of my deceased friend for the repast.

There were some older men there who were mockingly calling me *"Pastor!"* I remember feeling a little embarrassed, but I knew from early on that I would have to share in Christ's suffering and will have to face some of the challenges that he faced while he was here on earth.

You see Beloved, those men were unable to see the plans that God had and still has for me. They only saw the person they thought they knew, but something on the inside of me was stirring up and waiting to be birthed. Glory be to God! There is nothing spectacular about me but God has elected and chosen me for His purpose and His glory.

You are reading this book because the Lord has also elected and chosen you from the beginning. People's perception of you does not matter, and neither does how you view yourself. If it's contrary to what God says about you, then, it's a lie!

You see, I know first-hand that we have no choice in who God chooses to use. When God predestines you to do His will, there is nothing you or anyone else can do about it. You can't choose who God uses, not even if it is yourself. People may tell you that you are not called because you may not look nor sound the way they think you should look or sound.

But whose report will you believe? I encourage you to believe the report of the Lord! That report says Christ knew us and anointed us to preach before we were formed in our mothers' wombs. God has a plan for each and every one of us. Some are called to be led, while others — like you and I — are called to leadership.

CHAPTER 2:
The Narrow Gate

A Vision of Two Roads

Many years ago, before I surrendered my life to Christ, I had a vision of two roads. There was a smooth, nice, freshly tarred road and on the other hand — a hard, rocky, and unattractive road. I was at the entrance point of these two roads and had to make a choice. I wanted to escape the discomfort and delays on the narrow road so I chose the smooth road.

Before I could even take a step, I heard a strong but assuring voice from heaven say, *"Do not take the smooth road!"* The voice continued to say that the smooth road only looks good but will lead to death. *"Take the rocky road!"*

Even though what I heard did not make sense with what I was looking at, I obeyed the voice of God. Walking along the narrow road was very hard and at times impossible. I wanted to give up, but it was so dark that when I looked back, I could not see where I was coming from. I had no choice but to keep going. I walked until I ended up on a high bridge. There was a large body of water beneath it. The two things that I'm most terrified of are heights and large bodies of water, and there I was getting a vision of both.

I was so scared, that I was certain the bridge would be the end of me. At one point it started swaying from side to side, and I thought for sure that I was going to fall. I wanted to get off but I couldn't see its beginning or I could not see my hand in front of my face on the bridge, so I got on my knees and started to crawl.

Then suddenly I ended up in hell, and there was a spirit that was guiding me. The foul stench of burning flesh, mixed with the loud and gut-wrenching cries had me trembling with fear. I thought my worst fear had become my reality but kept following the spirit until I entered a field with the greenest grass that I had ever seen. The fresh scent of peace filled the atmosphere. Then the spirit said, *"Wait here for a while until you are called to go up to see God."* I exhaled and was filled with joy when I realized that my soul was not condemned.

I gave my life to the Lord soon after this encounter. Even though I was not living my life as a Christian, God still chose me and gave me foresight into my destiny. After receiving that vision, I was persuaded that no matter what hardship I go through, I will get through it just fine. We must go through some tough experiences, some that might seem unbearable. Metaphorically speaking we can compare these experiences as going through hell. Sometimes even in our relationships with family, friends or colleagues, we will experience disappointments and heartbreaks.

You see, there are two roads on this journey of life — the narrow way and the broad way. The broad way looks very smooth, nice and enticing. It seems like the right way to take. The broad way looks much easier to travel on as if you will get to your destination quicker and safer.

Meanwhile, the narrow way looks more difficult, unattractive, and painful to walk on. The narrow way is rocky and looks dangerously uncomfortable. It appears to be a long and tedious journey, and it seems as if it would take a much longer time to get to your destination via the narrow road.

> *"Enter by the narrow gate; for wide is the gate and broad is the way that leads to destruction, and there are many who go in by it. Because narrow is the gate and difficult is the way which leads to life, and there are few who find it."*
> **Matthew 7:13-14**

When you consider the two roads, the most logical choice would be the broad road, right? What if you could see what is at the end of the narrow road, would you choose to deal with the discomfort and rockiness now, to arrive at a better destination? Laying at the end of the broad way is destruction and death, but at the end of the narrow way is a beautiful gate that is ready to open to its new residents.

You won't need any special access code or identification to enter, because the fact that you made it to the end of the narrow way is proof enough that you are in the right place. We must take the narrow way no matter how long it takes, or how many times we get injured along the way!

While driving on the highway from work one night, and it started raining so hard that I could hardly see the road ahead. To make matters worse, one of my windshield wipers had stopped working. I was so afraid of getting in an accident, that I decided to take the next exit. I assumed the local road would be safer and easier, but it turned out to be a road of regret. The road was long, winding, and elevated with no barriers or walls. If I veered too much to the left or right, I would plunge to the darkness below!

So, I kept a slow steady pace all the while whispering the name of Jesus. By the time the road ended, I was shaking so much that I couldn't hold the steering properly. In that moment I had to completely trust God to take the wheel.

That's how we should navigate the road of life. As a preacher, you must lean on God and to trust Him to take control when the road gets dark, scary and lonely.

Sometimes life-altering interference and unforeseen circumstances can make us feel like we are going to succumb to our trials, but God gave us this assurance that our present trials and tribulations are not designed to kill us but instead to test us and prove us strong. There will be glory after this! Whenever you are doing anything in your life that will elevate you and make you better it always comes with a burden but when you have finished you will feel proud that you didn't give up.

CHAPTER 3:
The Correction of Love

This is what we speak, not in words taught us by human wisdom but in words taught by the Spirit, explaining spiritual realities with Spirit-taught words.
1 Corinthians 2:1

The Lord revealed to me through the Holy Spirit many things that have been a burden to him. The Lord showed me that some elected Preachers have been elected by his determinate counsel to walk in His precepts, but they are not truly serving Him.

Many are indulging in sexual immorality, fulfilling the lust of their flesh, and engaging in perversion. Many preachers are silently struggling with immoral sexual desires that are rarely addressed in the church. So, they are not getting delivered and are still preaching and leaving the pulpit to go back to their sinful lives.

This is an abomination to God. The Lord does not care about titles, positions, powers, nor social status. God cares about our souls. You must denounce every secret entanglement that you might find yourself in. Renounce all evil and unrighteousness and put your flesh under complete submission to the Holy Spirit and allow God to burn your flesh. The Lord has instructed me to write this message to those that are struggling with these stronghold spirits. You must submit that part of you and allow God to heal your diseases.

There is no affliction that the Lord cannot deliver you out of. Self-condemnation is a deadly spirit that can kill you spiritually and could lead you to die a physical death and cause eternal damnation. You may be able to still preach and operate in your calling while in sin. However, do not be deceived by this because the gifts and the calling of the holy spirit are without repentance.

You must allow God to work it out for you. You might sometimes still experience temptation while going through it, but you must continue to pray and trust the process. Believe that God can set you free from the bondage of that and all sin. Praying to God for forgiveness is not the same as repenting. Sometimes one can ask for forgiveness but then turn around and recommit the same sin that God has forgiven.

This is because it is easy to be led away by temptation, especially when it's a familiar sin that you have not yet been completely delivered from. But when you repent, you turn away from that sin. You no longer have the desire to do it because you have given it over to Jesus completely. God's grace is perpetual.

So, if we are not careful, we could sin presumptuously by going to God when it's convenient for us, but refusing to completely surrender to Him. The Lord forbids us to partake in lascivious behaviors (offensive sexual desires). These are sins that have been committed in the body, contaminating the vessel that hosts the Holy Spirit. Whenever we commit these sins, the Spirit of God can no longer dwell.

Therefore, we must put to death what is earthly in us, which are all evident works of the flesh: impure desires and passions, molestation and rape, orgies, fornication, homosexuality, adultery, and every detestable thing. God also warns us not to associate ourselves with people who engage in practices of sexual immorality. All sexual behavior such as those that are licentious, lewd, lustful and lecherous are demonic practices that displease the Lord.

Such practices are fruits that are conceived through sin that will bring forth both spiritual and natural death. These are sins that take place in the body and defile it, causing separation from God. The Holy Spirit lives inside of us so when we perform sexual acts we defile our bodies and become filthy and contaminated and thus, prevent the Holy Spirit from dwelling and reigning inside of us. The Holy Spirit cannot tolerate unholiness or function in such a vessel. He is holy, and so we too must be holy *(See Leviticus 11:44-45)*.

We must exercise our authority to be able to resist and rebuke the devil. Jesus was led into the wilderness to be tempted by the devil but Jesus rebuked him with the word of God. After many failed attempts to tempt Jesus, the devil had to leave. Matthew 4:1-11. The weapons we use to fight our warfare are not physical ones, but they are mighty and powerful by the word of God.

God's words are powerful and should be used when engaged in any spiritual warfare. Use the authority that God has given you to overcome the tempter. We have the authority to bind and loose elements on earth and God agrees to bind and loose those things in heaven.

There comes a time when every believer's faith will be tried. The testing of your faith is what makes you stronger spiritually. The trial of your faith also serves as a spiritual scale and will show you where you are weak or lacking. The Bible lets us know that all have sinned and fallen short of God's glory.

So, we know from scripture that preachers are people who have sinned and sometimes are still struggling. However, it is our responsibility to put to death every work of the flesh and put under subjection the things that can cause your entire body to be condemned. God is able to loose the bonds of unrighteousness and set you free from any stronghold spirit that you may t be wrestling with.

CHAPTER 4:
Preachers vs Pastors

Not everyone who preaches is a Pastor! Although many people use the terms interchangeably, there is a significant difference between the two. *Preachers* are ministers and servants of Jesus Christ. They are God's messengers who proclaim His word with divine authority. They function as great public speakers that evangelize and deliver sermons and also help to strengthen the faith of believers.

Most Preachers do not perform pastoral duties. However, some Preachers function and operate in both capacities. Preachers are God's heralds that exhort and preach the message of Jesus Christ to all who are willing to listen. The work of a preacher is vital to the body of Christ.

Usually, when we think of a Preacher, we imagine someone who may have come from an established family line of theologians and has inherited the gift through their bloodline. Another popular assumption is that the Preacher has gone through extensive studies themselves to attain a wealth of knowledge on how to preach.

While this may be true for some, this is not a requirement of God. Generally, preachers study the word of God and use it as a tool to exhort the Lord. They are empowered by the Holy Spirit, so they do not necessarily have to go to school for theology to be able to preach effectively. Knowledge is given to them by the Holy Spirit to edify and to bring spiritual healing to those that are sick.

Pastors, also known as shepherds, provide spiritual leadership to their flocks. A Pastor helps to shape and cultivate kingdom characters. They are like spiritual doulas who help to birth visions and push their flocks into purpose. Because of the magnitude of the mantle that pastors carry they rank higher than Preachers. Due to the complex and demanding nature of their role, Pastors must solely depend on the strength and power of God to work effectively.

I recently had a conversation with a young woman who had expressed to me her curiosity about Pastors. Her experience was that whenever she would visit a church, she would always become open and vulnerable; she exclaimed that felt safe and understood, and she was always in awe that Pastors were able to perform signs and wonders.

One can make a comparison between Preachers and Doctors. All Doctors retain the same title but many have specialized skills and serve special populations. Similarly, Pastors and

Preachers vary in their style, delivery and approach to carrying out their roles. Not all Pastors will appeal to everyone. Some are more effective with the youths, or the older congregants, for example. In the same vein, each Preacher has a specific sub-group of the body of Christ that he/she has been mandated and equipped to reach.

There are Preachers who have been preaching and indoctrinating the people of God with false teachings. Some are even preaching without first being appointed and sent out by God, but in doing so they are contradicting the doctrine and causing chaos and confusion in the body of Christ.

False prophets are on the rise deceiving as many as they can with religion, dogmas, divinations, and prosperity sermons. We cannot change this narrative, because it is written that in the last days these and many other deceptive things must happen. We must be very aware of the antichrist and the rise of false prophets. But we must not be deceived.

This is the reason why God said in Matthew 24:22: *"And except those days be shortened, there should be no flesh saved: but for the elect's sake those days shall be shortened."* Therefore; we must not allow these things to distract us nor make us ineffective in whatever we do for God! From the beginning of time until now, the people of

God have often chosen to hear soothing words instead of sound doctrine, their hearts have become hardened and despise the gifts of correction and wise counsel.

CHAPTER 5:
A Divine Call to Be Separated

There is a divine call for the elect of God to be separated from sin. When you are a leader the burden of proof falls upon you. The Lord has exhorted us to bring divine order to ecclesia, because this is where his judgments will begin first.

God has given us stewardship over his Church and it is our responsibility as stewards to see to it that the state of the Church of God is in right standing with God, and to also ensure that the affairs and operation of the Church are in the right order.

You must lead with diligence and with vigilant stewardship, always watchful. Be God's example and the face of what He requires His elect to look like, having that Godly confidence that you are well equipped and to complete your divine assignment with grace and with excellence. Holiness is a huge requirement from the Lord which means that we should not resemble the world so much that the Master would find it difficult to differentiate between the Church and the World.

We are Christ's authorized representatives in the earth, so it is our responsibility to walk in the ordinance of God, line upon line, precept upon precept. Do not be ignorant to the devil's devices that he has created to distract and deter you from walking in the way of the Lord. You must be bold in having godly confidence that the saving grace of Jesus Christ is enough to keep you free from sin.

You must be intentional about praying so you can truly overcome temptation, and live a holy life. This is required for you to have the full Holy Ghost experience in your life. God has given us strategies on how to pray because he knows what we need long before we even know we need it.

Throughout scripture, God gave many references to how His people should respond to sin. He suggests that we should also be separated from people that partake in sin. In Matthew 13 Jesus compares the kingdom of heaven to a field of wheat and tares. In the parable, the tares were planted together with wheat, and the owner of the field did not notice until they had both sprung up.

Tares are weeds that have a close resemblance to wheat, except for one distinct difference. The owner, not willing to risk uprooting the wheat, let both tares and wheat grow together until the time of harvest. In other words, because the field owner was unable to distinguish the good from the bad, he did not want to lose the good with the bad. Though the tares may look like the wheat for a season, the tares cannot bear the fruit that the wheat does. In like manner, God wants to separate His people to himself.

THRESHING FLOOR

I heard the voice of the Lord one day while I was in the spirit realm. He spoke clearly to me and said, *"Threshing floor!"* At first, my response was to panic because I automatically thought that it was a bad thing. Although I've heard of the threshing floor before I didn't understand the full purpose nor its significance.

I was afraid, thinking that I was in trouble with God, so immediately after I awoke from the vision I prayed and asked the Lord for the interpretation. The Holy Spirit revealed that God was calling me to a place of divine separation. I purposed myself to find out the meaning, use and purpose of the threshing floor.

The *threshing floor* is an ancient landmark that God has been using to demonstrate His judgments, love, blessings, and redemption. An Old Testament Prophet called Hosea prophesied that Israel would be "like the morning mist, or like the dew that goes early away, like chaff that swirls from the threshing floor or like smoke from a window" (See *Hosea 13:3).*

The Lord also used the depiction of the threshing floor to showcase his redemption in the book of Ruth 2 verse 20. Ruth was encouraged by her mother-in-law Naomi, to go to the threshing floor where Boaz was lying down for the night, and uncover his feet, to express her desire to be redeemed by Boaz.

To understand the significance of the threshing floor, you first must understand what a threshing floor is and its purpose. There are two main types of threshing floor: one is a flattened outdoor surface, usually circular and paved; meanwhile, the other is inside of a building with a floor of dirt, stone, or wood, where a farmer would thresh the harvest and winnow it.

The purpose of the threshing floor in its natural sense, is to serve as a place of separation, so that the grain can be harvested distinctly from the chaff (rubbish) or the inedible part of the grain that surrounds it. This process is performed by spreading the sheaves of grain out on the threshing floor and causing oxen or other cattle to tread repeatedly over them and loosening the barley, wheat and other grains.

Another process of threshing is called *winnowing which* also takes place on the threshing floor. *Winnowing* is when a winnowing fork (teeth shovel) is used to throw the mixture into the air, so that the wind can blow away the chaff, leaving only the good grain on the threshing floor.

The threshing floor also has a spiritual significance: it's a place where good and evil are separated. It is a place where the Lord separates those who truly love him from those who do not. God has called us from the beginning to be separated so it is very clear why he used the imagery and the depiction of the threshing floor to illustrate the importance of being separated.

We must be separated from sin by putting off carnality and by putting our flesh under subjection, and being confident that the blood of Jesus Christ is potent enough to wash off our sinful appearance so the glory of God can illuminate and outsource the powers of the darkness of this world.

CHAPTER 6:
The Do's of Preaching

"Woe to the shepherds who destroy and scatter the sheep of my pasture!" declares the Lord.
Jeremiah 23:1

But the Advocate, the Holy Spirit, whom the Father will send in my name, will teach you all things and will remind you of everything I have said to you.
John 14:26

You shall therefore lay up these words of mine in your heart and in your soul, bind them as a sign on your hand, and they shall be as frontlets between your eyes.
Deuteronomy 11:18

1. Pray

The Bible instructs us to pray without ceasing. Prayer is one way of giving God complete access and permission to move in the earth. It is also a major way that God communicates with man. Jesus demonstrated this throughout his journey, as he prayed often. (See *1 Thessalonians 5:18-18*)

2. Fast

Many spiritual benefits come from fasting. When you fast, you are starving your flesh to nurture your spirit. Fasting is also putting down your flesh for the glory of God and is necessary for your spirit to thrive. Fasting is so powerful it also benefits your natural body, by causing your body to pass out toxins. *(See Esther 4:16)*

It is important to fast as a Minister of the Gospel as fasting also cleanses and detoxes your spirit. In Mark 2 Jesus makes clear that once He departs from the earth His followers should fast. Fasting prepares your vessel to receive from the Holy Spirit.

When you fast, you receive the power to rule over your flesh. Jesus demonstrated this when he was led into the wilderness and was tempted by the devil after 40 days and nights of fasting. We see in Matthew 4 that He fasted and was empowered to resist the temptations from the devil. You will not be an effective preacher if you do not fast.

3. Commit

Commit your will to God's divine will for what He wants to accomplish through you in that service. You must commune with the Holy Spirit at all times for instructions. When you pray often, the Lord will reveal His plans, desires, and purpose to you. *(See Psalm 37:5)*

4. Study

Study to shew thyself approved unto God, a workman that needeth not to be ashamed, rightly dividing the word of truth.

2 Timothy 2:15

Study the word of God often so that when you are preaching the on-time *rhema* word of God, the Holy Spirit will bring back God's written word to your remembrance. When you read and study the Bible often, you are feeding your mind and spirit. The words that you've read will come to your mind and you will never forget them. This is why instead of merely *reading* the Bible we must truly *study* so that we don't take what the Lord is saying out of context and interpret it with our intellect and flesh.

5. Be Led by the Holy Spirit

But those that wait upon the Lord shall renew their strength; they shall mount up with wings as eagles; they shall run, and not be weary; and they shall walk, and not faint.

Isaiah 40:31

During the waiting period, something supernatural happens — spiritual elevation that takes place in the waiting process. The *wait* could feel like *weight*, which would consequently make it hard for you to embrace the joy and peace that comes. When you wait on the Lord you are subscribing to a continued renewal of strength with no end term date. Therefore, it is impossible to grow weary in waiting on God. Just wait!

As a preacher, you must wait on the Holy Spirit to give you utterance. Always ask the Holy Spirit to go before you, to the location where you are going to preach. It is very important to wait for the Holy Spirit to give utterance and guidance before speaking and moving. It is equally important for the Holy Spirit to lay hands on you before you lay hands on anyone.

When you're invited to preach at a church or on any platform, always pray and ask the Lord for His divine consent. Not every altar is of God so you must discern whether it is the will of God for you to serve at that altar before you agree and go. Otherwise, you risk operating without His covering and become subjected to whatever spirit is in control in that space.

Whether you have a mega-church or you're just preaching to loved ones in your living room, it does not matter! The location or size of your ministry should not be a factor in how submitted and obedient you are to God. In the book of Judges, we learn of Deborah, a prophetess and judge, who kept her ministry under a tree!

Aim to get to the place in your personal life and ministry, where you can reject some invitations without fear, and not be led by the expectations of man. When you are assigned by God to preach somewhere, the Lord knows exactly who is going to be there and what those people need. Wait on His guidance, instruction, and anointing always.

CHAPTER 7:

The Don'ts of Preaching

1. Never ask someone to pay for prayer or healing

When ministering the word of God to anyone, do not charge money or abuse your power and lead people to believe that redemption could be bought. As God's elect, we should not be a part of this blasphemy because God is not pleased with it. Salvation is a (free) gift from Jesus Christ to those who are willing to believe and receive it.

The gift is given to us who was once bound and lost and were redeemed by the blood of Jesus Christ. We must never be so proud and presumptuous to the point where we start charging people for something so tangibly divine and spiritual. The Bible tells us that angels do not understand because they are holy, supernatural beings that never sinned, thus they can't understand redemption. Christ did not die for them but indeed died for us. The prophets who were before us prophesied of this grace and they did search diligently to find it.

The Lord knows that you have needs and will always fulfill them. Jesus instructed His disciples in Luke 10 verse 4 to not bring any money bags with them. As a preacher, you will no doubt experience hard times but I encourage you to trust God.

But I rejoiced in the Lord greatly, that now at the last your care of me hath flourished again; wherein ye were also careful, but lacked opportunity. Not that I speak in respect of want: for I have learned, in whatsoever state I am, therewith to be content. I know both how to be abased, and I know to abound and to suffer need. I can do all things through Christ which strengthened me.
Philippians 4:10-13

When you are truly doing the work of God, the Holy Spirit will cause people to bless you without you asking. People will see the great works that God is doing through you and it will cause them to bless you. Let them do so freely. Do not exploit or otherwise manipulate the people of God for monetary, or any other personal gain.

There are times when the Holy Spirit might instruct you to sow a seed. This is a spontaneous event that should only happen when the spirit of God gives such a command. At that time you must not stand in the way of one whom the Lord has already laid it on their heart to sow and just might need that confirmation.

Acts 4 and verse 33-35 gives us this assurance:

"And with great power gave the apostles witness of the resurrection of the Lord Jesus: and great grace was upon them all. Neither was there any among them that lacked: for as many as were possessors of lands or houses sold them, and brought the prices of the things that were sold, and laid them down at the apostles' feet: and distribution was made unto every man according as he had need." As a servant of the Most High God you will never lack anything good. So, you won't have to ask or beg anyone for anything. As an elect of God, you were already predestined and commissioned to make disciples of all nations and to baptize them in the name of the Father, Son and Holy Spirit and to teach them to be obedient.

This should be your singular focus.

---

2. Never Sow nor Pay Anyone to Pray for You

Some people will tell you that in order for your gifts to be unlocked you must sow. This contrary to the word of God. Promotion only comes from God. Blessings do not cost a profit. When you give these so-called men and women of God your money to activate blessings or speak into your life, they consult with and receive power from the cast-down spirits, and in so doing they can bind you into that craft and can cause you to become dead spiritually and broke financially.

God is not pleased with anyone who sows to hear a word. Anyone who does this is under a satanic influence and is operating by the spirit of divination. The Lord says clearly in Acts_17:30 that_such a one should repent and renounce the practice of filthy lucre (money gained in a dishonorable way). God knows_your needs and promises to supply all of them according to His riches in glory. And guess what? We know that He can afford to fulfill this promise to us because all things were made by him.

In Psalms 50 verse 9 He states plainly that He has no need of a bull or goat from us His children, for every animal of the forest is His. The cattle on a thousand hills belong to Him. He knows every bird in the mountains, and the insects in the fields because they too are His. For the whole world is His, and all that is in it. He gave us all this detail so we would know that He is able to take care of us.

3. Do Not Engage in Witchcraft Practices

Witchcraft is a pagan practice in which evil spirits are summoned and inquired of to carry out certain assignments such as casting spells. The act of witchcraft is a ritual performance using black magic to execute diabolic plans against others to block their destiny.

Such powers come from demonic influence. When a person engages in witchcraft, that person enters into a binding contract with the devil. The devil is always so crafty in requiring something in return, which always results in sinning against God.

As God's elect, you are called out of darkness into God's marvelous light. Thus, you should not consult with any familiar spirit. Examine yourself carefully to ensure that you do not fall into the trap of witchcraft. When a person engages in communication with demons, they commit a grave sin.

In 1 Samuel 28, King Saul disobeyed God and so both God and His prophets cut off communication with Saul. Saul became so desperate for direction, that he sought out a witch for counsel. This displeased the Lord so much that He killed Saul and his sons the very next day.

The practice of witchcraft is ancient and still has the same negative impact that it had when it first came into practice. In order to split ties with this demonic world of witchcraft, you must seek God, denounce and renounce your affiliation with it. Though you will suffer for the sake of the Gospel as

Christ did, you must remain obedient to God, and not engage in evil works.

The Lord knows exactly what we are experiencing, including the temptations of your flesh. Remember there is no temptation that is common to us for which the Holy Spirit is not able to make a way of escape. But to escape, you must exercise your free will. You must have the zeal to do the will of God, and be able to put your body under subjection to the Lord.

---

4. Never Do Work to Be Recognized Or Praised By Man

"Be careful not to practice your righteousness in front of others to be seen by them. If you do, you will have no reward from your Father in heaven." Matthew 6:1 NIV

This is about your heart posture and intentions in doing the work of God as a preacher. Is it to please God, man, or yourself? God forbids us to do things to be recognized and exalted. All glory belongs to God, there is great reward in doing the works of God and in keeping his commands, but we must wait on Him to glorify us. Promotion comes only from God, and we must wait patiently on the Lord and he elevates us in due season.

5. Do Not Preach an Artificial Sermon

An artificial sermon is rehearsed or replicated. It has performance but no real power. There's a difference between preparation and planning exactly what to say, or copying another minister's sermon. Sometimes the Holy Spirit visits us while we prepare for a sermon, and we take notes immediately to avoid forgetting. However, in planning and preparing, always leave room for the Holy Spirit to move.

The Lord revealed to me that many preachers spend hours or even days writing out a sermon before a preaching engagement, and do not allow the Holy Spirit to direct their speech or delivery. Concerning this, the Lord is not pleased. Don't get me wrong there is absolutely nothing wrong with taking notes, but we need direction from the Holy Spirit who is the one who gives us utterance.

Proverbs 19 verse 2 cautions against hurrying ahead without knowledge, so we must always prepare ourselves to be called upon at any given time. Luke 14:28-30 *"For which of you, intending to build a tower, does not sit down first and count the cost, whether he has enough to finish it — lest, after he has laid the foundation, and is not able to finish, all who see it begin to mock him, saying 'This man began to build and was not able to finish'?"*

Too often leaders preach messages that entertain their listeners but do not edify them, so you might find that people may get excited by the message that has been preached but they have not truly experienced God. Whenever a preacher preaches without consulting and waiting on God for divine knowledge and instructions, that preacher is operating without God.

Be guided by, but not dependent on your notes when delivering a message from God. Always preach a *rhema* (on-time) word from God, which will surely accomplish God's will. As a preacher, commit to staying in the presence of God and continually open to the Holy Spirit's leading. This way you will never get caught unawares because of unpreparedness. Pray to God for His Spirit to fall afresh on you before preaching.

6. Do Not Engage in Spiritual Warfare on Social Media

We are in a time where social media has become a major marketplace to advertise and promote different businesses. Many people use social media as a tool to build their business and market their brand. As it turns out, many Preachers are using social media as a platform to preach the gospel. While it is a great vehicle to reach a lot of people across the globe, it could be a very toxic and dangerous place to get caught up in.

So-called preachers are using social media channels as a place to deceive the people of God with flattering and eloquent words. They speak in tongues to sound deep and profound. Many false preachers are using social media outlets as their main and only source of income, so they create content to keep their viewers entertained. This kind of content cannot edify, cover or convert anyone. In an effort to entrap those who have subscribed to their platforms, they will try to persuade people into thinking that it's alright to forsake the gift of corporate worship.

Some of these preachers use their platform as a place to mislead people into believing that worldly possessions are signs of blessing from God. There are witches and warlocks who also use social media as an outlet to mislead God's people under the pretense that they are prophets. They operate under the divination spirit to deceive as many as they can for monetary gain and fame.

Many false pretenders use social media platforms to troll others, they try to discourage other believers that are building according to the will of God. Sadly, we've seen and heard many testimonies of this vicious cycle repeating itself, In Nehemiah 4 we hear of Sanballat and Tobiah, who sent threats when they saw that Nehemiah was building the wall. They were angered at Nehemiah's progress and potential and tried to discourage him.

Many preachers who preach on social media are untrained and unlearned. They do not have anyone to hold them accountable, so they spew out the filth in the name of God

and contaminate the work of God. God is using social media and has called many to build His altar there.

There are a lot of people who are unable to physically attend church due to different circumstances who appreciate the opportunity to be able to hear the word of God being preached, and/or to receive deliverance right in their place of confinement. Wherever the name of the Lord is being glorified it must be a holy place.

God told Moses when he was up on the mountain, to take his shoes off because the Lord was there so it was holy. Even though social media is not a physical place, it is still a place where the people of God gather to lift up His name — a place of prayer and worship. Many souls perished because of the behavior they display on social media. God is watching us! Even when we think He is not there, He is still able to see our hearts and our actions.

You may not be in a building or have a large congregation but if God has assigned you to build an altar on social media, remain reverent and conduct yourself well. God is there! You must serve with diligence. Do not defile the altar of God, no matter where it is.

There is a remnant that awaits the manifestation of God. Our wayward sons and daughters are waiting on us to truly be delivered so they too can be delivered. The day is quickly approaching when we each have to give a report to God as to how we handled those who God entrusted to us.

7. Do Not Waste Oil

> *"Do not give what is holy to the dogs; nor cast your pearls before swine, lest they trample them under their feet, and turn and tear you in pieces."*
> **Matthew 7:6**

You have heard the saying don't cast your pearls before swine! Can a swine understand the worth of pearls? No, I tell you of a fact that a swine does not have the intellectual capacity to know what a pearl is, much less to know its value.

In Matthew 7:6 this is how God metaphorically describes it when we preach to unbelievers who refuse to listen. In the sermon on the mount Jesus warns his disciples not to waste time on hard-hearted people who would not value what is being offered, but instead would insult, mock, or attack them.

This parable_relates not only to non-believers but also to believers alike. Some believers go to church religiously and pretend to be holy. They have a form of godliness but when you tell them *thus says the Lord*, if it's not in alignment with what they want to hear they will reject and rebel against you. Whenever this happens do not force them to accept or receive you, by rejecting you they are rejecting the holy spirit that sent you by kicking against the prick. As an elect preacher, God will assign you to shepherd people that will not value what you offer, but do not be discouraged by this because as it is written a Prophet is without honor in his own country.

You might not deliver your message in the same way other preachers do. You might be directed by the spirit of God to preach a message of conviction that may not feel good to some and cause them to despise you. Nevertheless, you must preach in the order and fashion that the Lord leads. True repentance comes through conviction.

When you preach the undiluted word of God, it reaches the heart of the believers and causes them to open their hearts to receive the word that will then convict and convert them. Be wise! There is a remnant of people who are called by the name of the Lord who_is waiting to hear you preach the authentic word of God.

> *Because the creature itself also shall be delivered from the bondage of corruption into the glorious liberty of the children of God. For we know that the whole creation groaneth and travaileth in pain together until now. And not only they, but ourselves also, which have the first fruits of the Spirit, even we ourselves groan within ourselves, waiting for the adoption, to wit, the redemption of our body.*

Romans 8:21-23

We must use what the Lord has given to us to edify His people and to bring glory to his name. We will one day soon have to give an account of how we manage what we've been given. God must be pleased with our works because it is by our works that we will be judged.

CHAPTER 8:
The Authentic Preacher

And John answered Him, saying, "Master, we saw one casting out devils in thy name, but he followeth us not, so we forbade him because he followeth not us." But Jesus said, "Forbid him not, for there is no man who shall do a miracle in My name that can lightly speak evil of Me.
Mark 9:38

Many theologians today, just like the one whom John made mention of in Mark 9 verse 38, are imitating and trying to do what they see the true followers of Christ are doing. They have studied the Bible and can preach a good sermon, but they do not follow Christ. They have a form of godliness but deny His power to be transformed. Nevertheless, we must not waste any time trying to decipher who the Lord has called but instead test the spirit *(See 1 John 4:1).*

Never be intimidated by someone who is anointed to preach in a certain kind of way. Remember, the gifts and the calling of the Holy Spirit are without repentance. Allow God to nurture and prune you into His vessel to be used in whatever capacity His grace permits.

You have a unique sound that can and will erupt the earth's atmosphere and shake heaven's foundation when you surrender totally to God. It's not by might nor power but by the spirit of God. We are called to similar offices but each of us has a unique style, skillset and personality to use to deliver God's word.

God has intentionally chosen you, knowing what you have on the inside of you to advance the Kingdom. You do not need to imitate anyone to sound deep, when you spend time in the presence of God, He will give you prophetic utterances. Instead of impersonating someone's preaching style, wait for the Holy Spirit to give you your unique element and elevate you. It is said that to whom much is given much is required.

This means that if you carry a heavy mantle, God requires a heavy sacrifice from you. We should not simulate someone else's message delivery style, nor be envious of them. We do not know what sacrifice they had to offer to God to get that anointing and we may not be willing to make that kind of sacrifice.

God has given to every one of us a measure of grace, which is enough to do what He has appointed us to do. Abraham was willing to offer his only son Isaac as a sacrifice unto God, as a sign of complete trust and obedience. When the Lord saw Abraham's willingness to sacrifice his only son, God gave him a special anointing and he became the father of many nations.

It is also said that God gives us grace in measures, so we must be mindful of how we use it *(See Ephesians 4:7)*. If the Lord has graced you to lead a small ministry or a small group of people, you must be faithful with the little that God has given you until He graces you with more if He sees fit to do so. These basic principles will set the foundation for you to be an authentic preacher.

PREACH "THUS SAYS THE LORD"

The cry of God's people goes up before Him daily, and He's always looking for one that he could use to deliver His people. When you are led by the Spirit to preach in a church or ministry other than your own, He will give you the power to accomplish what He desires in that house.

When the Holy Spirit sends you to preach the word in a certain church and the leader of that church preaches differently from you, do not change to fit in with that leader's expectation or man-made standard of preaching. Be firm and uncompromising in the word God gives you.

Preach in the Holy Spirit and you shall see miracles, signs and wonders. Preparing for a sermon and not preparing for the Holy Spirit, could cause confusion. God is not the author of confusion so we know that such outcomes are not His desire.

A preacher must live according to these steps in order to be a successful one. When I say, *successful*, I am not talking about the treasures on earth that we store up. But instead, the treasures in heaven that no corrosion can corrupt, nor can any moth eat away. Fix your heart on the things of God because where your heart is, there your treasures are also. *(See Matthew 6:19)*

Let me use a passage from the Old Testament to illustrate my point. In 1 Kings 22. Ahab, king of Israel repeatedly rebuked and rejected the counsel of God. Ahab killed many of the Lord's prophets and also participated in idol worshiping. One day king Jehoshaphat, the king of Judah, visited Ahab. Ahab asked King Jehoshaphat to join him in battle against the Syrians, but Jehoshaphat insisted that they must first seek the knowledge of God concerning the matter.

So, Ahab brought 400 false prophets who all prophesied that God would give them victory over the Syrians, but Jehoshaphat identified their falseness and asked for a true prophet of God. Then Ahab sent a messenger to summon Micaiah whom he hated. Micaiah was hated because he always delivered God's truth to Ahab, which was often a message of rebuke. As he had feared, Micaiah prophesied and told him the truth that he would not get victory over Syria, this made king Ahab furious so he gave a charge to lock Micah up. Our God is gracious and merciful but God is also uncompromising.

As Christ's representatives and preachers of the gospel, we are obligated to preach the undiluted truth of God "Thus says the Lord." You must be completely obedient to God in speaking to whomever the Lord has instructed you to speak to regardless of their ranks and titles, even if it causes them to hate you.

However, you must give honor and respect to those whom the Lord has chosen and given charge to lead, regardless of their shortcomings. Only God is able to judge. You should always pray and ask God to help you go to that person in humility and tell them the truth, in love "thus says God."

According to Ahab, he hated Micaiah because he never prophesied good things to him. Notice that Micaiah never wavered, but still boldly spoke as directed by the spirit of God. I've had several conversations with people who when placed in a position like the one Micaiah was in.

They were fearful of being persecuted by leaders in the church, or by other powerful people. It is not unheard of now for people in church leadership to abuse their power by using it to control those who they are called to lead because they do not want to be held accountable for their actions or decisions.

We must never allow the fear of mortal man to let us fall into disobedience to God. Thus says the Lord — we must not fear the one who can only destroy the body but we must fear the Lord who can destroy both the body and the soul. Therefore, let us pass the time of our sojourning here on earth in fear and trembling.

SERVING AS A GUEST PREACHER

I was invited to pray at a church by the leader of that church. Prior to receiving the invitation, I had never met, nor spoken to the leader. She reached out to me through social media and told me that her church was hosting a 3-day shut-in and fasting service. She told me that on the second night of the service, the Lord appeared in a vision to a woman there. In the vision, the Lord gave the instruction that I should pray in the fasting service against the spirit of suicide that was upon the young men.

At the time of the invitation, I had never dealt with the spirit of suicide, so I prayed and asked the Lord to confirm the invitation to me. I was led by the Holy Spirit to Acts 16. In that chapter, Paul concluded that God had called him to preach the gospel to the people of Macedonia. After reading that passage, I was confident that the Lord had anointed me to pray in that service. When I arrived at the church, I did not know what I was going to say, but I had faith that the Lord would give me utterance.

In Act 16, while Paul and Silas were in prison a massive earthquake shook the prison doors open and all the prisoners were released. When the guard awoke and saw the chains and empty prison cells, he drew his sword and attempted suicide.

However, Paul told the guard not to harm himself. As I began to speak that same word came to me. God gave me the utterance to deliver the people that were there at the church with power and authority. I declared *"Don't harm yourself!" I said with conviction.*

Every spirit needs a body to operate legally in the earth realm and so when we pray, we are giving the spirit of God access to operate through us in the earth. When the Holy Spirit that lives inside of us begins to manifest, that's when the glory of God is revealed in us through miracles, signs, and wonders. Never take glory for anything that God empowers you to do.

There is a remnant of God's people that is hungry and thirsty for the undiluted, unpolluted, uncensored, unfiltered, and uncompromised word of God to transform their lives. They long to be redeemed from a life of sin, shame and guilt. Only the word of God when used with His authority and the anointing of the Holy Spirit can truly set people free and give them peace.

Sometimes you might feel that the very thing that God has called you to do won't be effective because of the magnitude of what he's placed upon you, but that is a lie from the enemy. If God called you to do something, He has already equipped you to carry out that assignment. Because of God's sovereignty, He's able to use even the ones that are struggling with self-doubt.

CHAPTER 9:
Never Compromise Your Anointing

Some people will ask you to pray for them to try and use your anointing for selfish gain. I was once having a conversation with a pastor, who told me that he prayed for a man who was facing criminal charges of child molestation. The pastor confided in me that though he felt that the man was guilty, he prayed for him anyway.

He petitioned God on the man's behalf for the judge to rule in his favor and dismiss the charges that were filed against him. After the accused man was found not guilty, the pastor glorified himself as the one who had personally caused the man to escape a possibly long prison sentence. The pastor expressed great disappointment that the man did not give him any money for his role in his acquittal.

The judgments of the Lord are just and sure. We should never pray and believe that God would let any sin go unpunished. Should he have prayed for him? Surely! But only if that man confessed his sins and has truly repented and is delivered from that evil; but if such a person does not want to truly be delivered then you as a leader might find yourself in err with God if you proceed to pray for someone in that manner. The integrity of your anointing must stay intact.

Whenever praying for someone who broke the law, he or she must confess, even if they have to face criminal consequences. Remember, you are a representative of Christ and not a defense attorney for criminals. There are people who will try to deceive you into interceding for them, knowing that they only want to receive from God but do not want a relationship with Him.

Never take bribery from anyone, as this is a blasphemy against God and could cause you to lose your anointing. Always consult with the Holy Spirit before praying for someone, to make_sure that there are no ulterior motives. When in doubt, pray that the Lord's will be done!

James 5 verse 6 says that *"the effectual fervent prayer of a righteous man availeth much"*. So, we know that there is power in our prayers, and they can produce results. Some people will come and try to bribe you to use your anointing to get them out of situations that God has willed them to be in.

If you attempt to pray for such persons, the conviction will fall upon you. Others will even try to be vindictive and ask you to pray for God to sabotage or kill someone. This reminds me of what happened when Aaron's sons Nadab and

Abihu, who offered up a strange fire before God and were punished to death for disobeying God.

To offer up a strange fire is to go before God with unholiness or unrighteousness. We must not go before God in flesh, but in Spirit and in truth. It is a very dangerous thing to use the gifts that God has given you for profit. Believe it or not, some people would try to buy your anointing. Never take money from anyone who tries to buy the gift of the Holy Spirit. Let's take a look at Acts 8.

This man called Simon was a sorcerer who deceitfully portrayed himself as a great man of God. After hearing the teaching of the kingdom of God and of Jesus Christ, he believed, got baptized and started following Peter. After some time, Simon offered the apostles money, saying he wanted to be able to lay hands on people so they will be filled with the Holy Ghost.

But Peter said unto him, *"Thy money perish with thee, because thou hast thought that the gift of God may be purchased with money...thy heart is not right in the sight of God. Repent therefore of this thy wickedness, and pray God, if perhaps the thought of thine heart may be forgiven thee."*
Acts 8:20

You cannot buy nor sell the anointing of God! It is a dangerous thing to use the gift that God has given you for filthy lucre.

Many other things can compromise your anointing such as gossiping and having an itchy ear. The devil will use people to call you with gossip to try and ensnare you. You must never fall for this trick. You must be able to discern and identify the spirit that is operating through such people.

Boldly rebuke the devil, as this a trap of the enemy to bring accusations against you. Do not give the devil a reason to accuse you. As a leader, you must be able to bridle your tongue. Do not listen to anything that is not productive, nor conducive to the move of the Holy Spirit. Stay away from idle conversations that will lead to sin.

CHAPTER 10:
The Importance of Faith

Now faith is the substance of things hoped for, the evidence of things not seen.
Hebrews 11:1

Faith is a powerful phenomenon that is frequently misunderstood. People often quote the popular scripture that is above. You must understand what *substance* is, in order to have a complete understanding of what *faith* is.

Substance is defined as *essential in nature*. Essence is a fundamental part or quality — it is the ultimate reality that underlies all outward manifestations and change. In other words, without any substance, there is no faith. To have substance, you must add value to the world, by thinking and doing hard work, and accomplishing something authentic and genuine — something real. You must work faithfully because faith without work is dead and vain.

What does it profit, my brethren, if someone says he has faith but does not have work? Can faith save him? If a brother or sister is naked and destitute of daily food, and one of you says to them, "Depart in peace, be warmed and filled," but you do not give them the things which are needed for the body, what does it profit? Thus, also faith by itself, if it does not have works, is dead. (See James 2:14-17)

We can see from this scripture that a man is justified by works, and not by faith only. Faith is an action word, requiring you to be proactive instead of reactive. It is always seeking employment and is always willing, ready and available to work for you. You must combine faith with work, in order to effectively complete your assignment. If you don't believe that God will do what you are petitioning him to do, then you are praying in vain.

God does not just want us to be prepared — He also wants us to be ready. When you pray for a particular thing, you must do the work to manifest that which you are trusting God for. Many people are going to hear about the works that God is doing through you and they will come to you for ministry.

Some will be bound by devils and come seeking deliverance. Others will be sick in their body and come seeking healing. Others will have problems and seek wisdom and counsel. In order for you to effectively minister to people in these ways, you must believe in God's power within you, and add works.

Faith doesn't just come by hearing, but it also comes by doing the will of God. Jesus said to the man whose son was possessed by demons that he must first believe. The man prayed and confessed his unbelief. Jesus rebuked the demon and immediately the boy was healed.

Throughout the entire Bible, it talks about faith, and how necessary and imperative it is to please God. Faith can move God to do the impossible. When your faith is being exercised and tried, you must also still believe that God is able to do what He promised despite what the circumstances say *(See Matthew 17:14-20)*.

Another biblical example of faith in action can be seen in the story of the woman who was bleeding for many years, and had exhausted all of her resources *(See Mark 5:25–34)*.
There was no hope for her. Then, she heard about Jesus and all the miracles he was performing so she found her way through the crowd to see Him.

The crowd was so thick that she went on the ground and crawled toward Jesus. Full of faith, she could only touch the hem of His robe, and immediately she was made whole. The woman's touch was of faith and because of her faith she was healed, God had no choice but to immediately respond to her faith because her faith was active.

GOOD VESSELS

You must be a good vessel. Therefore, you should not have any cracks, leaks or contamination that would prevent the Holy Spirit from using you to the fullest. A potter must put the clay through several different stages in order to produce the finished product. It is the same with us. God has to put us through a similar process, which I call *the trying process.*

As a good vessel, it is important to lay aside all offenses. Sometimes that will require you to forgive people who have wronged you and have not apologized. The Lord encourages us to forgive quickly so that we can do the work without hindrance. We cannot justify ourselves by holding those that offended us in our hearts. The law of God requires us to forgive all those who hurt us and that speak all manner of evil against us.

It is written that we must love those who hate us and in doing so there is great reward. It is unlawful and unrighteous to bear unforgiveness. It is said that when a sinner repents immediately all of their sins are_forgiven, but when a righteous man sins, if he dies, then all of his righteousness will be forgotten. So, we must not allow even the ones who offended us to cause God not to forgive us.

There was a woman who was bound with evil spirits and had sores all over her body. She was unable to eat and as a result was malnourished and unable to move, walk, or stand. Her family had taken her to many different doctors but none of them was able to treat or even diagnose her condition.

They became hopeless because she had been to many different churches and could not get her healing. The Lord had revealed to another minister that she and I should visit the sick woman and pray with her. So, we yielded ourselves to the Lord as vessels for the Holy Spirit to use, we fasted and prayed for many days.

We had to trust God completely that He had indeed sent us to bring healing and deliverance to the woman. As we began to use the word of God, I witnessed the power of God move through the woman's body that was debilitated and had been bed bound for months.

God still works miracles and has great work for His willing servants to do. When you submit yourself as a vessel to be used by God, He will work great miracles signs and wonders through you. Glory to God!

CHAPTER 11:
Graced to Complete, Not to Compete

I was in the realms of spirit one day talking with the Lord. As we were talking, I suddenly heard a loud roar. It sounded as if it was the voice of a man and of a lion, so I asked the Lord what the sound was and He answered and said these exact words to me, *"It is the devil going back and forth in the earth seeking whom he may devour."*

Then the Lord instructed me, *"Tell my people to drop their anchor. If they anchor down in Me, they cannot and will not be moved."* So, I obeyed the Lord and began to warn as many as I could.

There is a great evil that has infiltrated the body of Christ. Our adversary, the devil, has gained access through weak points such as jealousy, envy, insecurity and other gates. Through these gates, the devil has invaded the hearts of many preachers and deceived them. Many preachers have been ensnared, and are striving with others in hopes of gaining power and superiority. They have become lovers of themselves who see each other as rivals.

Wherever you would find competition, there will be division. This is a great offense that opposes the knowledge of God. Division brings desolation, destruction and ruin *(See Matthew 12:25)*. When you are truly doing the work of God you must never allow intimidation to overwhelm your heart, but instead you should be inspired and encouraged by others that are doing the same work.

Each of us has a unique ability to advance the kingdom, whether great or small. On the other hand, feeling inferior to others gives a false sense of inadequacy and insecurity. We should never think of ourselves more or less than we ought to, Refrain from exalting yourself or your gifts and talents.

In Genesis 4:6-16, God spoke of the two first sons: Cain and Abel. They were twins each having different gifts. Now, Abel kept flocks of animals, and Cain worked the soil. When it was time to bring sacrifices to the Lord, Cain brought some of the fruits of his land, and Abel also brought fat portions from some of the firstborn of his flock.

The Lord was pleased with Abel's offering, but not with Cain's. Cain became very angry and jealous. Then the Lord said to Cain, *"Why are you angry? Why is your face downcast? If you do what is right, will you not be accepted? But if you do not do what is right, sin is crouching at your door; it desires to have you, but you must rule over it."*

Cain became consumed by jealousy and resentment for his brother Abel. Even though God had warned him of what could happen if he allowed inadequacy to control him. When you are obedient to God and faithful with what He's given you, there is no need to compete or compare your abilities with anyone else's. We are workers together in building the kingdom of God. You may not be able to do the same work that your fellow comrades are doing, but it is important to know that He has given you the grace to complete and not to compete.

SOUNDING A CLEAR CALL

There is a divine order that you must follow whenever delivering God's word to His people. You should always minister the word of God with clarity. Sometimes when you are preaching, the anointing of God may come down and fill you up, and you will start to speak in tongues. There should be someone there to interpret, or you must interpret.

The point of this is to ensure that the congregation has clarity on what the Holy Ghost is doing at that time. When God sends a word for the church, it is better for the preacher to prophesy than to speak in tongues. If it is otherwise, the preacher will be edified and but the congregation will not be.

Before I gave my life to Christ, I had many experiences of visiting churches where pastors and other members would speak in tongues. I remember always feeling very confused. I felt out of place because I did not know nor understand what they were saying. They would speak in tongues throughout most of the service, even when they were praying for people. I would often leave the church feeling more isolated and lost than I was before going there.

It was not until I developed a relationship with God and had a personal encounter with the Holy Spirit, that I was able to speak, understand and interpret tongues. Preachers, your spiritual language is a gift from the Holy Spirit and should be used to exhort the Lord.

It cannot edify anyone else, especially if it's not being interpreted. When Jesus' disciples were speaking in tongues, the people that heard them thought that they were drunk. Peter had to explain the truth to them, and offer an interpretation. This understanding facilitated understanding and as the people opened their hearts, Peter prayed for them and they were all filled with the Holy Spirit *(See 1 Corinthians 14)*.

CHAPTER 12:
Ministry Tools: How to Handle Conflict & Affliction

CONFLICTS IN MINISTRY

Many unsaved people have had the unfortunate experiences of attending church, conferences and revivals and leaving the same way they went in because the word of God had been compromised. Preachers who practice what to say before preaching rarely get a chance to experience the move of the Holy Ghost. It is extremely important to usher in the Holy Spirit with true worship.

If you are having issues in your ministry, you should first pray and ask God for wisdom and guidance concerning the issue that you are experiencing. Do this before approaching anyone in your ministry regarding the issue. Never discuss the issues publicly in the time scheduled for preaching and deliverance, as the unsaved did not come to witness dirty laundry being aired. Always put God's business and priorities before those of mere men.

When behind the pulpit, yield to His will and let Him do and say through you what He wishes. Your job as a Preacher is to preach the undiluted and convicting word of God which is the truth. Failure to understand this basic principle is a reason why many churchgoers have not received deliverance, and many unsaved persons have lost faith in the church. I am a witness to that — I've seen it first-hand.

A few years ago, I attended the final night of a church's three days revival. The guest speaker was a man whose name had gone far and wide as one anointed in the gifts of healing and miracles. As a result, people with diverse kinds of sicknesses and diseases came out on that final night of the revival.

When I arrived at the venue, people were going up to the altar to share testimonies. A female pastor of the church went up to testify. When she went up to testify, another pastor who she was having disagreements with, came and grabbed the mic out of her hand. The Holy Spirit was not pleased and no one received their deliverance that night. God was wroth.

Pray and ask God for guidance in speaking to congregants or other leaders who you have an issue with. Your main purpose as a preacher is to win souls for Christ. Preaching the on-time word of God will cause people to repent and turn from their wicked ways so that God will be glorified. There is no conviction or power in a word that did not come from God. While that can cause an emotional reaction, it will not facilitate a supernatural encounter with God.

AFFLICTION IN MINISTRY

And as Jesus passed by, he saw a man who was blind from his birth. And his disciples asked him, saying, Master, who did sin, this man, or his parents, that he was born blind? Jesus answered, "Neither hath this man sinned, nor his parents: but that the works of God should be made manifest in him. I must work the works of him that sent me, while it is day: the night cometh, when no man can work. As long as I am in the world, I am the light of the world."
John 9:1-5

Do not make judgments against anyone that is experiencing sickness, or any tribulation. Some people are troubled in their bodies and in their minds with many different spirits and illnesses that they did not bring upon themselves. Some were born that way and will potentially be beneficiaries of God's powers of healing and miracles. When you do the work of God, there are souls attached to your ministry to be impacted through the Christ in you. Every soul is important to God and that is why you cannot afford to lose anyone that is attached to you.

The Lord has entrusted us to lead his people and in doing so he has equipped us with many spiritual gifts so that we can carry out the assignment. Do not think of yourself as better than anyone that is afflicted with an infirmity that God has led to you for prayer, but instead be compassionate when praying for them. We should treat everyone with dignity and love regardless of what the Lord might reveal to us about their condition.

We should always showcase the character of Christ whenever confronted. Do not judge nor condemn anyone no matter how long they've been in the condition that they are in. Christ has anointed and commissioned you to heal the sick and set the captives free.

This is a holy and powerful assignment that is to be handled with the utmost humility and honor. God exhorts us not to grow weary in doing well for people, no matter what the circumstance is.

As an elect of God, you were strategically chosen by God to manage and lead with diligence. We were once bound and appointed unto death but the grace of God redeemed us and so we must redeem our brethren. Jesus told Peter:

Simon Simon, satan has asked to sift all of you as wheat. But I have prayed for you, Simon, that your faith may not fail. And when you have turned back, strengthen your brothers."

Luke 22:3 NIV

We are the body of Christ having different members that work together cohesively to accomplish the same goal. This goal is to make ourselves available as ready vessels to be used for God's purpose and glory.

CHAPTER 13:
Breaking the Cycle of Church Hurt

There is a vicious cycle that has been plaguing the church for many centuries. More and more leaders with unresolved issues, hurt and unforgiveness in their hearts are leading ministries. As a result, they are inflicting the same kind of hurt on the ones they are charged to lead. Many leaders have left the church with bitterness, malice, and strife in their hearts, to then start other ministries without first being reconciled and healed.

Some of these leaders have even recruited other members to go along with them — they have corrupted the minds of their members against those they have been separated from. Often these decisions are made in rebellion and conflict, which results in division in the church.

The ministries of such leaders often contaminate and hurt the people of God. Subsequently, many people are turning away from the church now more than ever, people are leaving congregations at an alarming rate due to their traumatic experiences in the church. This form of trauma is often referred to as *church hurt*.

Church hurt is believed to be the worst hurt. Some people who have suffered this kind of hurt at the hands of leaders feel betrayed and rationalize their experience by saying that "hurt people hurt people." While that saying is indeed true for the world, it should not be so for the church. There is a balm in Gilead and it is for the people of God!

When leaders that have been affected by *church hurt* continue to lead others before they are healed, the ministries they oversee are usually negatively impacted. God is not honored by acts of revenge or rebellion, or our human attempts to prove things to each other.

This deadly demonstration is a mockery of the church which takes our focus off the souls that need to be saved. I believe that this is an epidemic that is happening worldwide and it is being organized and operated by the devil himself.

However, not all leaders who leave a ministry to set up their own are guilty of carrying bitterness and unforgiveness in their hearts and inflicting church hurt on others. There are some leaders that God has called out from under the leadership, to be shepherds of their own flocks. In most of these cases, God reveals this to both leaders.

In this situation, the leader who is called out must go to the leader that is over them and let them know what they believe the Lord had revealed concerning their assignment. Many leaders know the ones in their flock who are called to leadership and received confirmation from God before this conversation or split occurs.

Some overseeing ministers will even initiate the conversation with the one below them, and encourage them to step out in obedience. Whether the decision is met with a blessing or rejection, leaders should first and foremost obey God and accept His call for their life.

In order to be fit for service in the kingdom of God, you must go through training. The church is an institution that helps to prepare those who are called to leadership. There are times that God has to shift you to get you ready for the purpose that he has called you to. Sometimes the waiting process takes a while, but do not be discouraged to wait on the Lord. God knows what He has placed on the inside of you, and it must reach maturity before it is revealed. In His perfect time, He will elevate you and send you out.

If you are under the leadership of a ministry and God tells you that it is time to move on, you must do so with integrity and with dignity. Always give honor to the Man or Woman of God that poured into and covered you. Never start a ministry with impure intentions or hurt. Seek God first for healing, understanding and deliverance. Pray to God for a renewed mind and spirit so that you will shepherd those he has charged you to lead in love.

And no one pours new wine into old wineskins. Otherwise, the wine will burst the skins, and both the wine and the wineskins will be ruined. No, they pour new wine into new wineskins.
Mark 2:22

Leading a ministry with the wrong motives can cause unclean spirits to function and dwell in your ministry. In doing so, you may end up pronouncing curses and otherwise harming the people who you come into contact with. Some leaders use their positions and power to control their flocks.

These are occultic practices and should not be done in the house of God. Brethren, do not be like those who have done detestable things in the house of God, because they shall surely be judged and will go down to the pit, according to 1 Peter 4:17-18.

"For it is time for judgment to begin with God's household; and if it begins with us, what will the outcome be for those who do not obey the gospel of God? If it is hard for the righteous to be saved, what will become of the ungodly and the sinner?"

Those who suffer according to God's will should commit themselves to their faithful Creator and continue to do good. You cannot lead effectively in unforgiveness. Unforgiveness is a stronghold spirit that feeds off of your flesh and will suck the life out of you both spiritually and naturally. Why was it so important for Jesus to include forgiveness when teaching the disciples how to pray? It is vital for the believer to forgive, to be forgiven by our Father in heaven.

For God to forgive us, we must forgive our brothers and sisters that have offended us so that we do not repeat the cycle of serving the people of God with unforgiveness in our hearts. When we forgive it is not for the one who did us wrong, but it is for us. The offender may never admit that they've done you wrong and they may never accept your forgiveness but that's alright because you must truly forgive them in order to make offerings to God.

It is said in Matthew 5:23 that *if you are offering your gift at the altar and there remember that your brother has something against you, leave your gift there before the altar. First, go and be reconciled to your brother; then come and offer your gift. Reconcile quickly with your adversary, while you are still on the way to court.*

Never wait too long to fix it because you will give room to your adversary to accuse you, lay false charges against you, sow discord, and hinder your work. Satan is your adversary — he is your opponent and who speaks against you. Harboring unforgiveness in your heart will spread and consume your entire being. Choosing to forgive will release you from excess baggage that you've been carrying for a long time. You must break free from the spirit of unforgiveness.

CHAPTER 14:
Showcase the Character of God

I had the experience of taking care of an elderly couple. The husband was 90 years old, bed-ridden and unable to eat or drink on his own. I realized very quickly that he was slowly transitioning. I often held his hand and prayed for him. Though he was non-verbal, he would gaze into my eyes and grip my hand with a gentle but firm grip. I knew without a doubt that he had accepted and received Christ as his Lord and Savior.

One day when I was talking to his wife about Jesus, she told me that she was an agnostic. She believed that nothing is known or can be known of the existence or nature of God. She claims neither faith nor disbelief in God. As I continued to care for them, she watched her husband in agony, slowly fading away with each passing day. Soon, the man that she knew and loved for over seventy years was unable to recognize her, or communicate with her.

Their children had grown up and were no longer living with them, so her husband was all she had. As he grew weaker, she grew lonelier and sad. I knew then that I was there for a greater purpose, so I did not want to miss the opportunity to possibly win her soul for Christ. I became the comfort she needed by treating her with dignity, love and compassion.

Being well-equipped by the Holy Spirit and through my very own personal experience with grief, I was able to minister to her. I was honored that God had chosen me to be a witness of His grace and mercy, so I kept praying for her salvation silently in my heart every day. One day as I was ministering to her as I always do, she said to me, *"I wish I could believe like you do."*

Immediately, I prayed and asked the Lord to visit her and give her a personal encounter with Him. She often asked me questions about God, and when I told her about things written in the Bible, her face would light up with excitement and hope. You could see the inner man and subconscious man yearning and desiring to know the sovereign God.

If you ever get a chance to witness an atheist, agnostic or polytheist, minister to that soul as the Holy Spirit leads you. Remember that God does not desire that any should perish, but He also does not force anyone to believe in him. So, minister with gentleness and meekness. Preach the truth of God with grace and without compromising.

There is only one true God, who is King of all kings and Lord of all lords. He is the self-existent One and before Him there was none. The sovereign Lord is Alpha and Omega — the beginning and the end. We can only be saved by the blood of His begotten son, Jesus Christ. Amen!

THE SEVEN SPIRITS OF GOD

Isaiah foretold that the Holy Spirit would rest upon the promised Messiah, and that He would possess wisdom, understanding, counsel, fortitude, knowledge and fear of the Lord *(See Isaiah 11:2)*. As Jesus was blessed with these gifts by his Father, every believer is blessed with the same gifts by the Holy Spirit.

1. **Wisdom** distinguishes between right and wrong, seeks and upholds truth and justice, and balances personal good with the common good. In the Old Testament, wisdom is personified as a righteous woman, of love, protection, security, and supremacy *(See Proverbs 4:6)*. While in the New Testament wisdom is personified by Jesus himself, as pure, peaceable, gentle, of good conduct and full of Mercy *(See James 3:13)*.

2. **Understanding** is the gift of intelligence and enlightenment. It is the ability to perceive, comprehend, and interpret information; to have insight and discernment. meaning.

3. **Counsel** is good advice. It is the ability to teach and inform, guide and direct, warn and admonish, recommend and encourage. The Holy Spirit offers this special gift to parents, teachers, coaches, mentors, advisors, supervisors, elders, and the like. Counsel is not only the ability to give good advice, but to receive it as well.

4. **Fortitude** is an unwavering commitment to God or a proper course of action, and it shows itself as moral strength, courage, determination, patient endurance, long-suffering, a resolute spirit, stamina, and resiliency.

5. **Knowledge** is the ability to study and learn; to acquire, retain, and master a wide spectrum of information and put it to good use for constructive purposes.

6. **Fear of the Lord** is awe, reverence, and respect for God. It downplays human self-sufficiency and acknowledges that everything comes from God. Consequently, those who "Fear the Lord" gladly offer their praise, worship, and adoration to God alone.

7. **Piety** is the only gift not part of Isaiah's original list. Piety is personal holiness, the ability to live a decent life, free of sin, devoted to God, and obedient to God's will.

CHAPTER 15: Which Church Are You?

According to Revelations 1:11, Jesus appeared to John of Patmos in a vision while he was banished and in exile. He was the overseer of the churches in Asia and was ostracized by the Romans because of his powerful religious influence. In this chapter, God provides descriptions of the seven early Christian churches in Asia Minor, which is present-day Turkey.

These churches were named based on their geographical location. Jesus instructed John to write down what he saw on a scroll and send it to the seven churches throughout Asia. Jesus' message of correction and the judgment that is to come, also offers encouragement, hope and a promise of redemption to each of the churches. The prophetic letters serve as a forewarning to the present-day Christian churches so that we can weigh ourselves in the balance, and make sure that we are not found lacking anything.

1. Ephesus: known for having labored hard and not fainted, and separating themselves from the wicked; admonished for having forsaken its first love (Revelation 2:1-7)

2. Smyrna: admired for its tribulation and poverty; forecast to suffer persecution (Revelation 2:8-11)

3. Pergamum: located where 'Satan's seat' is; needs to repent of allowing false teachings. (Revelation 2:12-17)

4. Thyatira: known for its charity, whose "latter works are greater than the former", tolerates the teachings of a false prophetess. (Revelation 2:18-29)

5. Sardis: admonished for - in contrast to its good reputation - being dead; cautioned to fortify itself and return to God through repentance (Revelation 3:1-6)

6. Philadelphia: known as steadfast in faith, keeping God's word and enduring patiently (Revelation 3:7-13)

7. Laodicea: called lukewarm and insipid.

"He that hath an ear, let him hear what the Spirit saith unto the churches; To him that overcometh will I give to eat of the tree of life, which is in the midst of the paradise of God."
Revelation 3:14-22

CHAPTER 16:
Avoid Getting Burnt Out!

Is it possible for someone that's doing the work of God to be burnt out? Yes, it is! Being physically exhausted is very common in people who work rigorous and stress-related jobs. Leaders who have people-pleasing tendencies often take on more than they can handle to avoid disappointing others. Such persons are most likely to experience spiritual burnout, especially when they do not have adequate support to complete their workload.

The subject of exhaustion is seldomly talked about in the church because leaders are expected to meet the constant demands of the people they serve. The constant feeling of having many people and tasks waiting for your attention can be overwhelming and cause frustration. Burnout does not happen suddenly but is a subtle state that simultaneously builds up while reducing your energy level over time.

It causes you to be unmotivated, counterproductive, and complacent. The state of being spiritually exhausted is almost inevitable, but leaders should never allow it to prolong. Prolonged feelings of depletion, exertion, and anxiety can all indicate burnout. The loss of enthusiasm and the reluctance to commit to the work of God are also clear indications that you are experiencing burnout.

The state of being burnt out is a dangerous one to be in. It could lead you to become lukewarm and unwilling to complete your God-given assignment. The lack of zeal to do God's work is a trick of the devil, that will lead to slothfulness. Slothfulness is a sin of omission. God gives us strategies that we must apply to ourselves to avoid getting burnt out. You must prioritize, delegate, and set boundaries but most importantly, you must rest.

In *Exodus 18:13-19*, we see a biblical example of this. In this passage, we see that Moses served all day as a judge. Jethro his father-in-law inquired why he singlehandedly did this task. *"You and these people who come to you will only wear yourselves out. The work is too heavy for you; you cannot handle it alone."*

Rest is essential in the care of self. In certain professions, extended periods away from work are granted (sabbatical). The word *sabbatical* is derived from the word *Sabbath*, which is a day of rest dedicated to God. Leaders who understand the importance of spiritual sabbaticals, take the advantage of them.

Sabbaticals offer space for leaders to be still in the Lord and address their need for rest. In these cases, other leaders in the church are appointed to fill in with the duties. Ideally, those interim leaders might deliver sermons, or take the initiative to find preachers to minister sermons

Prayer To Unlock Your Potential & Activate God's Divine Will

Dear Lord Jesus, it's me, your child *(your name here)*.

According to Your word, eyes have not seen, ears have not heard, neither has it entered the hearts of man the plans that you have for me! (1 Corinthians 2:9)

I know that You've created me for Your divine purpose, and I am ready and willing to do what You've sent me here on earth to do. Lord, I know that I only have a set and limited amount of time to do it. I know that I will have to account for the time you've given me, so please help me to manage and utilize my time gracefully.

Lord, help me to accomplish everything that You've sent me to accomplish. Deliver me from the expectations of man. Help me to be mindful not to serve two masters. Deliver me from depression, overthinking, anxiety, confusion, exhaustion, inconsistency and every mind-controlling spirit. Deliver me from my Adamic nature and old ways of thinking.

Lord, I pray that my mind will be renewed each day. Help me to break free from the spirit of religion, false doctrines, dogmas and traditions. Lord, teach me how to love and trust you completely and to be submissive to Your will. Teach me how to put away trivial things and be more Kingdom-minded.

Help me to lay aside every burden that has been weighing me down. Please help me to live a life that's fulfilling and rewarding. Lord, I pray that I will be fruitful and have great substance. Teach me Lord, how to bear the fruits of the spirit. Lord, I understand that dying without fulfilling Your purpose for my life would be a great tragedy. So, please help me to maximize my fullest potential.

You said in Your Word that I should not be anxious for anything but with prayer and supplication and with thanksgiving that I should make my petition known unto You. Teach me how to pray more and worry less. Deliver me from stress and anxiety. Lord, I pray that you will reveal my purpose to me, and empower me to walk in it.

Lord, I know that the loneliness I feel sometimes is not the absence of people but it is the absence of purpose in my life. But Lord, I believe that you will manifest your purpose in me. Lord, I believe that when I find my purpose, the fulfilling relationships that I seek will come. You said that my gifts shall make room for me, and I believe every word You said about me. So help me to wait on You to lead me into my purpose and into destiny relationships.

Your word says that You have plans to prosper me and to give me good hope and a future. Let those plans come forth, Lord God. I accept your divine will for my life. I pray that I will no longer allow doubt, disobedience, fear, peer pressure, procrastination, slothfulness, disappointments or any outside influence to control my destiny.

I renounce and denounce everything that my adversary, the devil, has said about me that is contrary to the words that you spoke over me. I renounce and denounce every word curse that I have come into agreement with knowingly or unknowingly. Let every yoke of bondage and every evil altar that is working against my destiny catch fire now, and. I bind every demonic spirit that has been assigned to delay, derail or destroy my destiny.

I cancel and destroy every diabolical assignment against my life and purpose whether it be obeah, juju, black magic, white magic, chakras, necromancy, voodoo or witchcraft. I cancel every plan of the devil against me. Let my angels pursue now every evil worker that is working against me, my family and my purpose. Lord, let there be confusion now in the camp of the enemy.

Let my enemy's foot be caught in the net that they set for me. Let my enemy fall in the pit that they've dug for me, Lord. I cast down and demolish every altar of darkness that was set up as a barrier or is being used as a barricade to block my progress. I blind the eyes and deaf the ears of every supernatural or human agent of the devil sent out to monitor my progress. I shut down every demonic surveillance that is working against me.

I decree and declare that I will manifest every plan and spoken word concerning my life. I decree and declare that no weapon that has formed or is forming against me will prosper. I decree and declare that every plan of the enemy against me will work together for my good. I decree and declare that every curse, limitation and sickness in my bloodline will stop with me. I decree and declare that no bloodline curses will be passed down to my children.

I claim my entire family for You now Lord, and ask You to put Your mark upon us. In me oh Lord, You have built your church and decreed that the gates of hell shall not prevail over me. Let it be so according to Your word. Let every hidden plot that is being developed to come against me or to come against the fulfillment of Your purpose in my life be voided, nullified and exposed. I cancel all premature death assignments against me and my family.

I declare that my children and I shall live out all of our days. Lord, I believe your word is true! Let the angels that You have given charge over me be released now to stand guard over my place of rest, business, school and vehicle now, in the name of Jesus Christ of Nazareth! I command my destiny angel to bring forth my answers now concerning my purpose.

Lord, let your purpose and divine will be done in my life as it is heaven. Let every gift that You have placed inside of me be manifested now. I use my divine authority to enter the spirit realms and bring forth into the natural everything that You have pre-destined for me to have. I decree and declare that as of today, there will be no more satanic delays or setbacks.

Lord, release the breaker anointing over my life, to break every chain and prison bar that has kept me in bondage.
Lord, release Your mighty and resurrecting power and let every dead and dormant area of my life that is keeping me out of Your will come to life now, in the name of Jesus Christ of Nazareth!

Lord, I know You despise lukewarmness so let the fire of Your Holy Spirit ignite me and set me on fire for You. Lord, I ask you to renew my strength and give me hinds' feet so I can be surefooted and run the distance. I decree and declare that I will flourish in every land that my feet tread.

I decree and declare that I will no longer cast my pearls to the swine. I decree and declare that I will not squander my inheritance. I decree and declare that my worst days are behind me and that my best days are ahead of me.

I decree and declare that I will live a victorious life. I will live in the overflow, and walk in the power and favor of my God. I decree and declare that not only will I see the promise but I will live in it. I decree and declare that I will enjoy the fat of the land that is flowing with milk and honey. I decree and declare that I will walk in newness and into the promises that the Lord my God has made to me and to my forefathers.

I decree and declare that everything that is mine and everything attached to me will be prosperous. My family is blessed. My finances are blessed. My ministry is blessed. I decree and declare that as of today I will walk in my Identity! I reclaim my rightful authority as a royal priesthood, a peculiar people, and a holy nation. I decree and declare that I am a child of the King and my life, my thoughts, my home, my identity and my mindset will reflect it!

God, I know that you are a covenant keeper. I decree and declare the blessings of Abraham upon my life, and the life of my children, and my children's children. Lord, I know that you are not a man that You should lie nor the son of man that You should repent, so I believe and I come into agreement now with everything that You have said concerning me.

All these I pray in Jesus' mighty and holy name.

Amen!

www.ingramcontent.com/pod-product-compliance
Lightning Source LLC
Chambersburg PA
CBHW050655160426

43194CB00010B/1946